Turnaround

**Renewing organizations
small or large
from the inside out**

To order copies of this book,
or to learn more, please visit:
TurnaroundMinistryLeader.com

Thirty-six years ago I sensed God's call to train leaders in Christ's church. For almost four decades, God in His sovereign grace has allowed me to serve as a church planter, a senior pastor, on staff at two wonderful congregations, an educational administrator, a full-time professor, a denominational executive, and a regional denominational president. In these varied roles, I have worked with ministries that were thriving, as well as organizations that were on the verge of collapse. For some people, chaos and crisis are a warning foghorn that says, "Keep away!" For me, they are a dinner bell. Others run away; I run toward—eager to make a difference. While it might seem crazy to some, I have been most fulfilled when I was used by God to bring renewal and revitalization to an organization.

It is against this backdrop that I humbly submit this book on turnaround ministry leadership.

Dwight A. Perry

April 2012

Every person has a foundation—a beginning that helps shape not only who they are, but the legacy that they leave to the next generation. My foundation was my loving, God-fearing, dearly departed mother, whose love and prayers undergirded me no matter how difficult the challenge I faced.

Mom, I know you are dancing with your Savior now in heaven, but I miss you every day. Thanks for laying down your life for me and my brother, especially as a single parent in the inner city of Chicago. I love you and dedicate this book to you.

Love,

Your son,

Dwight

I would also like to thank Dwight Clough for his assistance in transforming an unedited document into this finished book. See DwightClough.com.

Good ministries fail.

Sometimes churches, megachurches, parachurch organizations, and/or whole denominations find themselves in crisis or decline even though they are doctrinally sound, spiritually energetic, and divinely commissioned. Or sometimes they plateau. Like the airliner that loses its engines at 35,000 feet, the passengers may be unaware that anything is wrong. But the pilot knows. Something needs to be done very soon, or the flight will come to an unscheduled and unpleasant conclusion.

Leaders need to do more than just steer the ship. Though the waters may seem smooth, they need to see the iceberg ahead shrouded in fog. When they do, they need to reverse their engines and rescue their people from calamity. Like the men from Issachar[1] who understood the times and knew what Israel should do, leaders need to read the signs of organizational disease and know how to bring it back to health.

Turnaround ministry leaders value the good of the people they serve above their own personal

---

1   1 Chronicles 12:32

preferences. They find the courage to take the risk needed to bring their ministry back to health.

Whether you are a pastor of a local church, a mission's executive, a denominational leader, or a lay leader on a church or parachurch board, this book was written for you. It does not give you an easy three-step solution to your ministry's crisis or decline. Instead, it will equip you with the tools you need to assess your organization's health and determine the appropriate steps needed to bring renewal and revival.

Contents

Chapter One

Inheriting Disaster: The Story of Dr. Joe

You may find yourself at the helm of a ministry that stands on the brink of decline. I've certainly been there, and most leaders will be there sooner or later in their career. Whether you pastor a local church, sit on the board of a mission, direct an educational institution, or lead a parachurch ministry, your ability to weather storms and bring your ministry back to health will be tested. It's only a question of when.

To help you understand the process of turnaround ministry leadership, I want to introduce you to Dr. Joe Green, a fictitious character whose experience parallels my own[2]

---

2 In 2004 I left my secure position as a prominent faculty person at one of the nation's leading bible colleges to assume the role of a denominational executive. Years earlier I had served on the national staff of this same denomination. I knew the ins and outs of denominational leadership, and I had promised myself never to go back into this type of work again. But the call of God was not something that I could run away from. As a result, I found myself in what our denomination considers the

and that of other leaders with whom I've worked.

Dr. Joe was one of the top leaders in his denomination. He had served as a church planter, pastor, educational administrator and bible college professor. As he approached his fifties, he asked God for the final chapter in what had been a long and fruitful career in vocational ministry. Little did he know, however, what that final chapter would look like.

His denomination, the Baptist Brotherhood of America, had been in a search for two and half years for a new District Executive Minister (DEM) to serve and oversee the ministry of the district to its more than 100 churches. Dr. Joe's name had come to the attention of the search committee, who initially could not believe that he would even have an interest in this role. The DEM job is seen by many as the most unrewarding role within Dr. Joe's denominational structure. These executives are the closest link one layer up from the local church, but due to the polity of the Baptist Brotherhood of America, they hold limited authority, in certain situations, to revoke ordinations and ministerial credentials issued by the denomination—even withdraw a church from the de-

---

most pressurized, but least understood, role in our entire structure—a District Executive Minister.

nominational group tax exemption by disfellowshipping it. Despite this positional power, most lead by influence and relationship. Challenges for a DEM abound. The DEM is sometimes blamed by the churches for things he has no control over and can be pressured by the national denomination to implement programs that make no sense to the local churches he serves. The typical length of term for a DEM is less than ten years. If a DEM comes back for a second five-year term, it means his district is making progress. If he stays for ten years or longer, he is considered a saint.

The DEM role had been vacant for two and a half years when Dr Joe arrived to fill it. For approximately eight years the district had been in turmoil. What Dr. Joe did not realize was this: Deep and divisive were the issues that were on the verge of destroying this 120-year-old organization.

A week after his formal installation, Dr. Joe discovered that the organization he was charged with leading was a quarter of a million dollars in debt. A week after that, filled with a mixture of excitement and trepidation, he attended his first meeting with his governing board.

After exchanging pleasantries, Dr. Joe got straight

to the point: "I recently met with Vice President Sam Fundraiser who has informed me that we, as a district, are in debt by a quarter of a million dollars. Here are the signed contracts by the former DEM. Were any of you aware of this?"

Bruce Pastor, the chairman of the board, spoke up, "This is the first I've heard or seen any of this." What followed was a robust and very intense conversation. "How did we get in this place?" "What are we going to do?"

After the board meeting was concluded, Dr. Joe met with Chief Financial Officer Shelly. "Shelly, we need to get on top of this issue. Please set up a process by which we engage these churches who have made pledges to our district. Where are we in terms of those commitments? Are the churches following through?"

Soon after this board meeting Dr. Joe met with his staff to discuss the situation. "We are in a fragile place," he said, "not only because of the financial issues but also because of the division that has taken place over the prior seven years between more established churches and the new churches."

Over the next couple of months, Dr. Joe commissioned a team of leaders from around the district to help him and the Board clarify the vision of the district. This process took almost six months and culminated in a two-day meeting at one of the churches.

Meanwhile, it didn't take long for Dr. Joe to get push back on his desire to address this, as well as other issues that had led to the breakdown of the ministry of the Baptist Brotherhood of America. During these first six months, Dr. Joe found himself increasingly involved in unresolved issues from the past that had literally sucked the life out of the organization. One of first things he had to do was terminate one staff person and pull the plug on the funding of another staff person who was very popular within the district. Many days he felt overwhelmed and underappreciated. He sometimes wondered if he had made the right decision to leave academia, with all of its perks. Now he was trying to manage a crisis that seemed to be unraveling faster than he could keep up with.

A clarified vision helped. However, before it could be implemented, another staff termination was required. Furthermore, when the district's headquarters moved to a different city, a long-time staff person did not feel led to transfer with the organization. These transitions, especially the termination of senior staff, left Dr. Joe even more discouraged. By this time he had been in his position a little less than two years, and the finances of the organization were only slowly beginning to turn around. The district was no longer running deficits, but the long-term stability of the organization was still very much in doubt.

Dr. Joe was giving it everything he had. Between work-related travel and the work itself, a ninety-hour week was typical. Then the unthinkable happened. Dr. Joe was diagnosed with a rare type of cancer. Any despair he felt was now compounded. Every day he questioned whether or not he had made the right decision to take this assignment. Upon finding out about the cancer, he called for a districtwide conference call, where he frankly shared the details of his health journey.

Up to this point, Dr. Joe had met life's obstacles head-on and overcame every one. He was no stranger to challenges. Almost from birth, he was fighting to overcome. Born and raised in the inner city of Detroit, he was six years old when he watched his father beat up his mother. When he was seven, the family found his father in the arms of another woman. Divorce followed, together with a move to his grandparents' home. Although he and his family lived in the inner city, the inner city did not live in them. His mother and his grandparents pushed him to go beyond his circumstances. As a result, he escaped the snares and temptations of his neighborhood, and went on achieve success in athletics and academics. Pushing forward, he graduated from one of the top universities in the nation. After coming to Christ, he went on to become the first African American to earn a Ph.D. from one of the leading evangelical seminaries. His ministry career defied the odds, overcoming the challenge of race to rise to leadership within a predominately white evangelical context.

But now Dr. Joe faced an obstacle he could not simply overcome. He was at the end of his resources. Here was something that could not be accomplished apart from God's grace and God's power.

This was the turning point. A 90-hour work week was no longer possible. The rhythms of Dr. Joe's life were changing. Instead of forging ahead, as he was accustomed to doing, he was forced to pause, to listen to God, to seek counsel, to see God in deeper way. Every moment became precious. Each opportunity was approached with focused intentionality. Prayer became central. It was no longer Dr. Joe plowing forward. A new dependence on God and partnership with others emerged.

No one is saying this was a painless process. Dr. Joe walked through valleys of deep discouragement and doubt. But he came out on the other side. And, as he emerged into the sunshine, the organization he was charged with leading began turning around as well. This district of the Baptist Brotherhood of America was no longer in decline—no longer in jeopardy of collapse. Vision was clarified. By year four, the district was no longer in debt. By year six, it was operating with a healthy and appropriate surplus. More importantly, by the end of the second year, people who hadn't been talking to each other for years found a new respect and appreciation for one another. By year three, friendships were being forged among the leaders in the district. By year five, the district was one of the leaders in the denomination in new church starts. Established churches were growing, and the working relationships between the churches and the denomination had never been better. Other independent churches were applying for membership in the denomination. Members of this 100+-church network stepped up to the plate to carry forward the new core strategic initiatives that had been developed.

Dr. Joe became what you also can become: a turnaround ministry leader.

How did he do it? How did Dr. Joe take an organization that was facing collapse and get it to thrive once again?

The rest of this book will explain the principles Dr. Joe employed. These are principles. We're not talking about a three-step program that only works in certain situations with certain types of ministries. Instead, these principles work for any ministry—church, parachurch, mission, or school —experiencing crisis, plateau or decline. They are listed in order of priority and implementation.

Chapter Two

Hitting Rock Bottom: Coming to the End of Your Own Resources

Turnaround is our responsibility as leaders

Turnaround ministry leaders are used by God to bring their organizations out of a downward spiral. Every ministry—just like every individual—faces the possibility of plateau and decline. Without proactive intervention, an organization torn apart by crisis, or lulled to sleep with apathy, will die.

Many leaders don't even know the early warning signs that their ministry is tipping toward decline. To begin to understand this, we need to take a look at your ministry's life cycle. Just as the human body goes through stages, so also will any organization. All of us are born, we grow and peak, and then we begin to maintain and eventually decline.

However, there is an important difference. With the human body, eventual death is certain.

Organizations can be renewed for decades—even centuries, if leaders know what they are doing. Martin Saarneen of the Alban Institute writes, "We must understand at the outset that the life cycle of a church has very little to do, if anything with chronological time. ... It has to do with the relationship and balance of certain 'gene structures' common to organizational life."[3]

A Ministry's Life Cycle

Maturity **Maintenance**

Growth **Decline**

Birth **Death**

A Ministry's Life Cycle[4]

To put it another way: Are you trapped by the

---

3 Martin F. Saarinen, *The Life Cycle of a Congregation* (Herndon, VA: The Alban Institute, 1986), pg 4.

4 Based on "Organizational Life Cycle" by Pinnacle Ministries. Used by permission.

organizational life cycle? If the chart says you're in decline, are you stuck there? Absolutely not![5] In fact, getting ministries out of decline is a critical part of your calling as a leader.

Vision drives ministries through a successful launch, past the attendant start-up risks, and into the growth phase because the leaders and the team are outwardly focused—functioning as a team, flexible, and willing to make the sacrifices needed to see the vision fulfilled. But when the team becomes self-absorbed and inwardly focused, the members slip into maintenance mode, forgetting to move forward. Instead, they cling to past accomplishments, entitlements—outdated and irrelevant procedures that cause them to slide into conflict, decline and, barring intervention, death.

Your job as a turnaround ministry leader is to

---

5 In my regional denominational context, God has been greatly using the Retool Kit Pathway to help the churches I serve understand that the organizational life cycle is not inevitable from birth to death. To put things back on track, leaders and those they serve must be willing to reassess their vision based on their God-given calling and the changing needs of the people they are seeking to reach. This outstanding renewal process was coauthored by Rev. Gary Harrison and Rev. Ray Swatkowski of Pinnacle Ministries. More information is available at http://pinmin.org/ministries/the-retool-kit/ (accessed 9 March 2012).

recognize these signs, and to take appropriate action to reverse the decline and pull the ministry out of maintenance, back into growth.

As servant leaders, we have a paramount responsibility to see that Christ's Great Commission is fulfilled until He so chooses to come back to claim His precious Bride, the church. We must do all we can to present His Bride back to Him, holy and spotless, for it is the church—specifically the local church—that He has chosen to use to win a lost and dying world back to Himself.

Yet, if God doesn't show up …

To carry out this incredible responsibility, we leaders must start here: No matter how well we plan, no matter how brilliantly we execute, turnaround won't happen without God. Ultimately, God must turn the organization around. The prophet Zechariah put it like this, "Not by might nor by power, but by My Spirit,' says the LORD of hosts."[6] Turnaround leaders understand that, if God's power doesn't flow through broken people, all our hard work will accomplish nothing.

---

6 Zechariah 4:6 NASB

Lessons from Elijah

The story of Elijah confronting the prophets of Baal[7] illustrates this key truth. Under the leadership of King Ahab, Israel had turned away from her God and drifted into apostasy, worshiping the false god Baal. Then Elijah the Tishbite, one of the settlers of Gilead,[8] showed up on the scene. He predicted that there would be no rain in the land, no doubt bringing to mind the covenant curses[9] that promised a lack of rain if the nation of Israel turned from God. All along, God was preparing the prophet Elijah to demonstrate to all Israel that Yahweh, not Baal, was still the one and only true God. After predicting the drought, Elijah went into hiding. While hiding, he restored a poor widow's son to life. This miracle served as another sign that God, Yahweh, was greater than Baal or any of the other false gods of the land. All of this happened despite Elijah's shortcomings.[10]

Eventually, Elijah was called out of hiding. He confronted King Ahab. The narrative reads:

---

7 1 Kings 18
8 1 Kings 17
9 Leviticus 26:18-19, Deuteronomy 11:16-17, 28:23-24
10 He later ran from a woman (Queen Jezebel) and, in a state of overwhelming depression, even asked God to kill him. See 1 Kings 19.

Ahab went to meet Elijah. When Ahab saw Elijah, Ahab said to him, "Is this you, you troubler of Israel?" He said, "I have not troubled Israel, but you and your father's house have, because you have forsaken the commandments of the LORD and you have followed the Baals. Now then send and gather to me all Israel at Mount Carmel, together with 450 prophets of Baal and 400 prophets of the Asherah, who eat at Jezebel's table."[11]

Ahab gathered these false prophets and prepared, at Elijah's urging, a burnt offering with two oxen, proposing a test to see who the true God was. The narrative continues:

So Ahab sent a message among all the sons of Israel and brought the prophets together at Mount Carmel. Elijah came near to all the people and said, "How long will you hesitate between two opinions? If the LORD is God, follow Him; but if Baal, follow him." But the people did not answer him a word. Then Elijah said to the people, "I alone am left a prophet of the LORD, but Baal's prophets are 450 men. Now let them give us two oxen; and let them choose one ox for themselves and cut it up, and place it on the wood, but put no fire under it; and I will prepare the other ox and lay it on the wood, and I will not put a fire under it. Then you call on the name of your god, and I will call

---

11 1 Kings 18:16b-19 NASB

on the name of the LORD, and the God who answers by fire, He is God." And all the people said, "That is a good idea."[12]

I will not go any further into the details of the narrative, except to say that, even though Elijah was outnumbered, despite the ridicule he no doubt endured, and even though he looked like an outmatched fool, it was the God of the Bible—the God of Israel—who showed up and showed to the rebellious people of Israel who really deserved the title, "God."

Kingdom success is not wedded to popularity. Instead, it is tied to God's name.

Insights from Watchman Nee

Years ago, I read a book that changed my life, *The Release of the Spirit* by Watchman Nee.[13] The premise of the book is simple: God must break our outer man (our mind, will, and emotions) in order that His Spirit might be released through our inner man (man's spirit). Living in this fallen world, we tend to rely on our five senses (our body) and our soul (mind, will, and emotions, or

12 1 Kings 18:20-24 NASB
13 Watchman Nee, *The Release of the Spirit* (Indianapolis: Sure Foundation Publishers, 2000).

how we relate to the outside world). This is all the natural man has. Prior to receiving Christ, our spirit—the part of us that relates to God—is dead.[14] It cannot understand the things of God[15] until the Holy Spirit invades our spirit when we put our reliance in Christ. Even though, at conversion, we put our trust in Christ for our eternal salvation, our ability to experience the fullness of this salvation while here on earth is directly related to how broken our outer man (mind, will, and emotions) is in terms of our ultimate trust. Prior to coming to Christ, we are forced to make sense of life through our thinking, our emotions, or our habits (will). When we trust less and less on our own intellect, emotions and willpower, and more and more in Christ, we begin to experience Him in His fullness.

How does this inner brokenness typically take place? God gives us circumstances that are beyond our control and beyond our ability to fix. In times like these, we learn not to rely on our own competence, intelligence or leadership ability. Instead, we fall on our knees and cry out to God.

Can you come to the end of yourself without going

---

14 Ephesians 2:1
15 1 Corinthians 2

through some type of life transforming experience? I'm not God, and I don't know. But the Bible is full of stories of people, from Joseph to Peter, who were thrown into situations that were too big for them to handle alone. Even Jesus sank to His knees and said, "... not My will, but Yours be done."[16]

The psalmist said it like this, "The sacrifices of God are a broken spirit; A broken and a contrite heart, O God, You will not despise."[17]

Lessons from other leaders

Nothing is accomplished without prayer and humility.

John Hyde was known as a man who could get things done—on his knees. As a missionary to India over 100 years ago,[18] he prayed so long and fervently that the floor near his bed was marked with hollowed out places where his knees rested. Known as "Praying Hyde," it is said that his heart even shifted out of place because of his times of intense and fervent prayer.

The impossible remains out of reach until we tap

---

16 Luke 22:42 NASB
17 Psalm 51:17 NASB
18 Hyde lived from 1865 to 1912.

into God's power, Paul said:

> Blessed be the God and Father of our Lord Jesus Christ, the Father of mercies and God of all comfort, who comforts us in all our affliction so that we will be able to comfort those who are in any affliction with the comfort with which we ourselves are comforted by God. For just as the sufferings of Christ are ours in abundance, so also our comfort is abundant through Christ. But if we are afflicted, it is for your comfort and salvation; or if we are comforted, it is for your comfort, which is effective in the patient enduring of the same sufferings which we also suffer; and our hope for you is firmly grounded, knowing that as you are sharers of our sufferings, so also you are sharers of our comfort.

> For we do not want you to be unaware, brethren, of our affliction which came to us in Asia, that we were burdened excessively, beyond our strength, so that we despaired even of life; indeed, we had the sentence of death within ourselves so that we would not trust in ourselves, but in God who raises the dead; [19]

> ❝ *True brokenness can only be experienced when we realize in our experience that, unless God intervenes, we will not be delivered.*"

---

19 2 Corinthians 1:3-9 NASB

My own story

For years, I relied on my ability to get things done in my own strength. Coming out of a broken home, growing up in one of the worst neighborhoods in the country in the 1960s, I overcame much and achieved much. Starting out as a high school football star, I went on to earn several degrees and became the first African American to earn a PhD from Trinity Evangelical Divinity School. I walked around thinking that hard work would overcome any obstacle.

Not until I faced a life-threatening disease did I experience a situation in which hard work would not prevail. No matter how hard I worked, I could not overcome this. This was humbling. This was discouraging. This was overwhelming. But, through this experience, I finally began to understand what the Apostle Paul meant when he wrote to the church at Philippi, "I can do all things through Christ which strengtheneth me."[20]

Jesus said it like this:

> "I am the true vine, and My Father is the vinedresser. Every branch in Me that does not bear fruit, He takes away; and every branch that bears fruit, He prunes it so that it may bear more fruit. You are already clean because

---

20 Philippians 4:13 KJV

> of the word which I have spoken to you. Abide in Me, and I in you. As the branch cannot bear fruit of itself unless it abides in the vine, so neither can you unless you abide in Me. I am the vine, you are the branches; he who abides in Me and I in him, he bears much fruit, for apart from Me you can do nothing."[21]

Some translations use the word "abide." That word "abide" means to remain, to dwell, to live. Jesus is telling us that no matter how much knowledge, skill, or ability we might have in and of ourselves, lasting fruit only comes as we remain connected to Him through the word of God and prayer.

In my case, He had to use a life-threatening disease to bring me to this place, possibly because of my extremely strong will. In the course of my battle with cancer over the last several years, I have firsthand experience of what the Apostle Paul termed "despairing of life."[22]

Please do not misunderstand me. I am not saying you must contract a life-threatening disease before you can come to the end of yourself. But I am saying that, somewhere in your journey, God will use His word, circumstances, and/or other

---

21 John 15:1-5 NASB
22 2 Corinthians 1:8

people to bring you to this place of inner brokenness.

As a Christian leader, you are responsible under God for the health and fruitfulness of your ministry. Your ability to see this become reality, however, will only take place when you come to the end of your own resources and learn how to abide in the Vine.

One leader said it best, "Descending downward is the key to greatness."[23]

Brokenness in the life of God's chosen leaders produces the type of life that transforms an organization from the inside out. Do you want to turn your ministry around? Start from the inside. Invite God to do whatever it takes so that He can flow through you.

Pause to Ponder

As you reviewed the organizational life cycle, what stage would you say most characterizes your particular church or organization?

---

23 See Bill Hybels and Rob Wilkins, *Descending Into Greatness* (Grand Rapids: Zondervan, 1994).

Describe a particular period in your life when it seemed like your life was falling apart. What did you learn from that period of time? Did the experience draw you closer to, or further away from, God? Why or why not?

What is your response to the quote, "True brokenness can only be experienced when we realize in our experience that, unless God intervenes, we will not be delivered"?

Chapter Three

Understand the Context

"He who gives an answer before he hears,
It is folly and shame to him."
Proverbs 18:13 NASB

As a leader, you need to understand how things are connected. Simple example: If the children's ministry volunteers in your church never receive any praise from the pulpit or any form of appreciation, expect trouble when you go to recruit more volunteers. The two things are connected. Likewise, ministry crisis and decline is always connected to a context. Problems don't take place in a vacuum. As a leader, you need to be tuned into those connections so you can make intelligent decisions about how to turn things around. You need to understand your context.

Listening is a critical part of this process. It's tempting at times to come up with answers before we even know what the question is. But turnaround leaders discipline themselves to slow down and listen. They learn to ask questions, draw out information, gather intelligence, use assessments, and arrive at a clear strategic understanding of the context.

The sons of Issachar

In 1 Chronicles 12, we read about the mighty men who assembled to help establish David as King of Israel. In the middle of the narrative, we read, "Of the sons of Issachar, *men who understood the times*, with knowledge of what Israel should do, their chiefs were two hundred; and all their kinsmen were at their command."[24]

Out of nowhere, it seems this comment about the sons of Issachar is dropped into the narrative. On face value, they were not as impressive as some of the other tribes listed. But they stood there because they were able to do two things: (1) The Hebrew word translated "understood" is derived from a verb that literally means to discern, perceive, observe, pay attention, or understand.[25] These were individuals who knew how to listen

---

24 1 Chronicles 12:32 NASB, emphasis mine
25 See Warren Baker and Spiros Zodhiates eds., *Hebrew-Greek Key Word Study Bible* (Chattanooga, TN: AMG Publishers, 2008).

well to those around them and arrive at an understanding based on that information. (2) They not only understood what was going on around them, but they also had the ability to give sound judgment and counsel as to what Israel needed to do.

What does this mean? This means that your context is always in motion—always changing. Yesterday's context is not today's context. In the biblical example above, there was a moment in time when supporting the reign of Saul was God's plan. That moment came and went. A new moment, and a new king, had arrived.

Ministry approaches change over time. For example, when I first started out in full-time ministry, Sunday Schools were the rage. Publishing houses were at their peak, and the Sunday School was seen as a key strategy to increase the growth of the congregation. Today, Sunday Schools are all but dead. Now everything revolves around small groups and life group interaction. When I came to know Christ, programs such as Evangelism Explosion were on center stage. Groups like Campus Crusade for Christ and the Navigators were making confrontational evangelism the norm. Today, confrontational evangelism, while it still has a place, is overshadowed by relational evangelism. Likewise, your ministry's strategies will change because the times change. The message of the gospel stays the same, but it will be communicated differently to each generation. Not only is this true, but the rate of change is increasing. What worked five years ago may not be appropriate today. More than ever, turnaround ministry leaders must understand the times.

Understand the culture of your ministry

In Carolyn Weese's *The Elephant in the Boardroom*,[26] a book that addresses the issue of pastoral transition, we find four chapters that are worth the price of the book. These chapters describe the four cultures of a church. Every church, every ministry, every business, every organization—whether religious or secular—has a culture. As a turnaround leader, you must understand the culture of your ministry. If you do not, your attempts to bring about growth and fulfillment could be met with unmovable resistance and resentment.

Every church, whether rural or suburban, inner

---

26 Carolyn Weese and J. Russell Crabtree, *The Elephant in the Boardroom: Speaking the Unspoken about Pastoral Transitions* (Hoboken: Jossey-Bass / Wiley, 2004).

city or affluent, belongs to one of these four cultures. The culture will dictate how decisions are made and how the people will process any leadership you provide.

While these cultures apply to churches, they also apply to other ministries and organizations.

Family Style Culture

In a Family Style Church, decisions are made based on relationships and how the decision will affect others. Informal networks such as friendships, longevity of the relationships, and being in the same family have a great bearing on how the mission gets accomplished. The predominate theme in a Family Style Church is that decisions should be processed very carefully, lest someone get hurt or be disappointed. The pastor or the leader is seen as the benevolent dictator. He/she must, above all else, shepherd the flock and care for the spiritual needs of the people as paramount. Knowledge is passed down based on relationships. Relationships trump almost any other value.

Archival Culture

The Archival Church depends on a central source for information, dogma, and doctrine that is passed down as the primary standard for truth and order within the fellowship. While the Family Style Church is focused on present relationships, the Archival Church looks to the past to see what practices, dogmas, and rituals prescribed by their forefathers must be continued. Archival Churches, then, tend to be oriented toward the past, rather than the future—or even the present. Spiritual authority resides not so much in the leaders as it does in the rituals, ordinances, sacraments and/or doctrinal statements of the church.

Iconic Culture

Iconic Churches revolve around a central personality. Many of today's megachurches within American evangelicalism are Iconic churches. A central leader dominates the focus. For example, if I asked you to tell me the name of Joel Osteen's church, you might not know. But, when I mention the name "Joel Osteen," nine out of ten people know who he is. He is an Iconic leader. The ministry depends on the presence of the leader to succeed.

Replication Culture

Unlike the relationship-driven Family Style culture, unlike the tradition-focused Archival culture, and unlike the personality-centered Iconic culture, the Replication model is the most future-orientated model. It puts emphasis on developing reproducible systems that can translate the mission of the particular church or ministry into a viable growth pattern of effectiveness. A Replication culture insists on putting systems in place that can guide the church moving forward, regardless of who the leader is.

Determining the culture of your particular church or organization is paramount if you are going to be effective as a turnaround leader. Tools such as the Natural Church Development (NCD),[27] or the Retool[28] process, and skills such as critical listening and strategic questioning will help you identify your ministry's underlying culture.

---

27 See http://www.ncd-international.org/public/essence. html (accessed 16 March 2012)

28 http://pinmin.org/ministries/the-retool-kit/ (accessed 9 March 2012)

Should you seek to change the culture? Sometimes the only way to achieve a vision is to change the culture. For example, a Family Style Church begins to break down at about 300 people. Beyond that, a Replication Style Church is needed to sustain growth. But the process of changing your church culture can be strewn with mines. Get advice before you set out to change your ministry's culture.

Location—Your outside cultural context

Understanding the cultural context of your church or ministry not only involves understanding what takes place on the inside but also—and just as importantly—the cultural context of the area where your ministry is located, or the area you have identified as your ministry's target area.

When my wife and I bought our second home, we were so excited—not because it was a fancy home (it was not), and not because it was a huge home (it was not). We were excited because of the location. One of my children suffered from severe learning disabilities. We moved from a school system that we could see was taking him down a path of destruction. When we moved to

Homewood, Illinois, heaven on earth opened up for us (at least, that was how it felt.) The Homewood schools were exceptional, especially their special education program.

Location, location, location!

Location was the critical variable. Just like understanding our current context in terms of meeting the needs of my child drove us to make one of the best decisions in our lives, so also understanding your ministry context provides the background for how you will move your organization from decline to growth.

Understanding the cultural context in which you minister is more important than ever before. During the 1960s and 1970s, the evangelical church flourished here in America as it became more proficient in delivering high quality programs and worship experiences to an already churched culture. This churched culture had been raised within a context where the Bible was still perceived as a holy book, even if you did not agree with it—where going to church was part of the socially acceptable fabric of society. Denominationalism was at its peak. This is no longer the case in America. The culture has shifted dramatically in the past fifty years. Our culture has moved from church-friendly to church-averse. What worked in the past does not work today. Like the GPS unit that finds itself heading off in an unexpected direction, we need to recalibrate. We need to move from merely being effective pastoral leaders to becoming effective missional leaders. Thinking like a missionary is no longer reserved just for persons who serve overseas. It is just as critical for those of us who serve Christ here in the United States. America has become the fourth largest mission field in the world. While our culture was once rooted in Judeo-Christian values, it is more and more rooted in all types of secularization, mimicking the path of modern Europe. Author David Hesselgrave encourages us to see ministry through the lens of a missionary ministering cross-culturally.[29] Perhaps this is why Ken Callahan writes, "The day of the professional minister is over; the day of the missionary pastor has come."[30]

Understanding the cultural context of your ministry is not a step that can be neglected. Recently, a church sent me a wonderful proposal

---

29 See David F. Hesselgrave, *Planting Churches Cross-Culturally: North America and Beyond* (Grand Rapids: Baker Academic, 2000).
30 See Kennon L. Callahan, *Effective Church Leadership: Building on the Twelve Keys* (Hoboken: Jossey-Bass / Wiley 1997).

for how they were going to address one of their major areas of weakness. The church had plateaued and was beginning to decline. The proposal was solid in every respect except one: It failed to define and communicate how it was going to impact the unchurched in their community. It even failed to identify who they were trying to reach and how they were going to reach them. By failing to address these issues, the church had not constructed a plan that would be sustainable because the church must minister to their world, or the church will not succeed.

Understanding your cultural context takes time. Even though I have been in Converge Worldwide (formerly Baptist General Conference) for over 23 years and in my current role as Executive Minister of Converge Great Lakes for eight years, I am just now understanding the cultural context of Converge Great Lakes and how that contrasts to the context of the district I came from in the same denomination, Converge Mid-America.

A helpful assessment tool The Percept Group[31] provides an immediate snapshot of your cultural context. This organization will help you identify both the demographics and the psychographics of

31 http://www.perceptgroup.com/ accessed 14 March 2012

your target group or location, allowing you to better understand how your target culture thinks and makes decisions. Their service is affordable, and they now offer an online interface that allows you to get the information you need within a few minutes. Their highly readable reports are filled with charts and graphs addressing population, household composition, race, ethnicity, gender, age, income, population by phase of life, census, marital status, family structure, transitional populations (college, military, homeless), education, occupation, employment, poverty and retirement income, housing, transportation, lifestyles, ethos, faith involvement, religious preference, leadership preference, primary concerns, key values, and household contributions.

As helpful as the Percept Group is, there is no substitute for spending personal time with individuals and groups within your target area. Hearing their story first gives you and your ministry the right to be heard.

Four disciplines that will help you understand your context The following four disciplines will help you understand your ministry's context:

Discipline #1: Approach every situation without forming a premature judgment. James spoke to the saints who had been "dispersed abroad," saying, "... everyone must be quick to hear, slow to speak and slow to anger."[32] James could have been talking to me, especially during the first 50 years of my life and the first 25 plus years of my ministry. I was always quick to form a judgment. I was always quick to give an opinion—even when one was not asked for—and I was always quick to not only give an opinion but to act like it was the only right one being offered. Instead of being a person who was QUICK TO LISTEN, I was quick to speak. But God has been transforming me into a person who is quick to listen. Like me, you may need to discipline yourself to approach every situation without forming a premature judgment. Listening gets you to better solutions faster because you invite others into the problem-solving process and unearth creative paradigms that you might otherwise miss.

Discipline #2: Follow a defined protocol. Before you make a decision, make sure you have followed some type of prescribed, well-thought-

---

32 James 1:1,19b NASB

through protocol. When the writer of Proverbs says, "He who gives an answer before he hears, it is folly and shame to him,"[33] he is encouraging us to follow a process—to get our facts straight before we make a decision or say something we might regret. Reactionary leadership is not turnaround leadership. We need to be people of process.

In the ministry I serve, people joke that when you hear the name, "Dr. Perry," you will hear the word "protocol" right after it. At first that annoyed me, but now I rejoice that the people who I have been called to lead understand that we follow a well-thought-out and fair process to arrive at our decisions, even if some disagree with the final decision.

Protocol doesn't exclude God. On the contrary, good protocol invites God in at every step and gives Him the supreme right to intervene at any time, and in any manner, He wishes.

What is a protocol? It's merely a process of decision making that is based on experience. In other words, we learn from past mistakes and use a process that prevents us from making those same mistakes again. A protocol gets better results. Adhering to protocol shows that you are a

---

33 Proverbs 18:13 NASB

disciplined leader. It shows that you are prepared to take input from all sides before making a decision. It gives those you lead the confidence to know that you are not going to simply make some type of arbitrary decision but will be careful to hear the voice of God when you decide.

Discipline #3: Use objective tools. Make sure you use outside objective tools in your assessment. All of us are good at making hunches and, to be honest, some of us are really good at, so much so that most of the time we are right. But such individuals are rare, and leaders tend to overrate their intuition. Balance your hunches with solid data. Use as many objective tools as you can to help form your opinions. Successful ministry leaders rely on objective data to get a clear picture of what needs to be done.

Discipline #4: Pray. Prayer is not something that we do in order to get God to bless what we already want to do. It is the key tool you and I have as believers to engage the heart of God so that it becomes our heart. As such, it is by far the most important aspect of any discernment process.

Consider these verses: "Be anxious for nothing, but in everything by prayer and supplication with thanksgiving let your requests be made known to God. And the peace of God, which surpasses all comprehension, will guard your hearts and your minds in Christ Jesus."[34] Also, "and this I pray, that your love may abound still more and more in real knowledge and all discernment, so that you may approve the things that are excellent, in order to be sincere and blameless until the day of Christ."[35] And don't forget, "Delight yourself in the LORD; And He will give you the desires of your heart."[36]

In other words, as we delight in God, He, by His grace, will put in our hearts the desires that will bring Him maximum glory and us the greatest good. Turnaround leaders make prayer preeminent in the discernment process.

Avoid these mistakes

There are some factors, however, that hinder us from being able to understand and discern our context clearly and accurately.

---

34 Philippians 4:6-7 NASB
35 Philippians 1:9-10 NASB
36 Psalm 37:4 NASB

Bringing our own bias into the process Pre-understandings, or pre-biases, that are not brutally exposed up front can sabotage the discernment process. Years ago, I taught a class at Trinity Seminary. One day I stood up and boldly proclaimed, "All of us preach heresy." As you can imagine, these fine evangelical urban ministry students were caught off-guard. But then I explained, "No matter how well-trained or how disciplined we are, we come to the biblical text with certain pre-understandings that will cloud our understanding of God's word unless they are brutally and honestly laid bare." For example, I grew up in a 20th Century Western culture, not a First Century Middle Eastern culture. But the New Testament was written within the context of a First Century Middle Eastern culture. Therefore, I need to be careful that I do not read into the text my 20th century pre-understandings.

Neglecting protocol As I mentioned earlier, I am often kidded about how everything in Dr. Perry's grid must come out of some type of protocol or process. Please don't get me wrong. I do not want to reduce the work of the Holy Spirit down to some sterile type of process; however, God

Himself is a God of order, and He is not the author of confusion.[37] When you seek to gain understanding by using a time-tested assessment process, you will make better decisions based on better data. Adhering to protocol helps you hear God better.

Neglecting prayer Prayer is your first priority. After almost four decades of ministry, I am convinced more today than ever before that prayerlessness leads to carelessness.

Let us be like the men of Issachar who understood their times. Become a person who understands the context before you implement any type of plan. This will help you become a turnaround leader who sees the power of God unleashed.

Pause to Ponder

Out of the four cultures described in this chapter, which one is most closely aligned with your church or organization?

---

37   1 Corinthians 14:33—"confusion" is sometimes translated "disorder"

Do you agree with the author that understanding your cultural context is critical for you as a turnaround ministry leader? Why, or why not?

What have you, as a leader, done over the past year to understand your cultural context?

Chapter Four

Create a Sense of Urgency

A couple of years ago I needed to take a physical to obtain life insurance. (Gone were the days when I could just show up and get the insurance I needed.) During the examination, I stepped on the scale. Lo and behold, my weight had shot up to 260 pounds. I was shocked. Because I carry my weight well, it didn't show. To others, and to myself, I looked like I was around 220. But I wasn't. The reality of this added weight, together with high blood pressure and the attendant possibility of a stroke or a heart attack, came as a wake-up call for me. I was shocked into action. Not only did I change my eating habits, but I also did the unthinkable for this old football player. I hired a personal trainer. This investment of time, energy and money kept my goal of losing weight on the forefront of my mind and heart. As a result, my weight went down, and my fitness went up. I am eternally grateful for the sense of urgency that caused me to take action.

Would I have made any of these changes if I hadn't seen "260" on the scale? Probably not. In the same way, your ministry will not make changes unless you, as a turnaround leader, are able to create a true sense of urgency.

John P. Kotter, author of *Leading Change*, puts it this way, "Establishing a sense of urgency is crucial to gaining needed cooperation. With complacency high, transformations usually go nowhere because few people are even interested in working on the change problem."[38] He adds, "By far the biggest mistake people make when trying to change organizations is to plunge ahead without establishing a high enough sense of urgency."[39]

What keeps your ministry from deteriorating and sliding into plateau, decline and death? You, as a leader, must continually refine vision and mission, and communicate it with a corresponding sense of urgency.

No matter what business or ministry you are in, people gravitate toward the normal and avoid the radical. Change comes hard. Please don't

---

38 John P. Kotter, *Leading Change*, (Boston: Harvard Business Review Press, 1996), p. 36.
39 Kotter, p. 4.

misunderstand me. I do not endorse change for the sake of change. I don't believe in inventing crises that don't exist. But understand that complacency breeds decline. Unless you, as a leader, recapture and refocus your mission, your organization will lose traction.

Creating a sense of urgency within your ministry does not mean creating a false crisis, but it does mean you must be committed to creating a culture of truth and accountability. Turnaround leaders view reality not as an enemy to avoid, but as a friend to embrace. Unfortunately, many leaders downplay the truth in an effort to keep people happy. But we must understand that being a friend means telling the truth, even when it hurts. The writer of Proverbs says, "Faithful are the wounds of a friend, but deceitful are the kisses of an enemy."[40]

You make reality your friend by keeping before the people you serve the specific needs of the people your ministry is called to reach. Don't allow yesterday's accomplishments to blind you to the needs of today. Keep your focus outward and missional. Inward and self-centered leadership does not reach people for Christ. Churches particularly must constantly revisit this truth. *It's*

---

40 Proverbs 27:6 NASB

not about us. Many churches that are three years old and older stop reaching the unchurched. That is tragic. We are in ministry because people don't know Jesus and, ultimately, because our God cares about a world that is desperately sick, and He wants us to reach the people He loves.

Here are five principles you can use to create a healthy sense of urgency in the lives of the people you are called to lead:

Principle #1: Tell and retell the story. Your ministry exists for a reason. You're trying to reach someone. Tell that person's story, and keep on telling it. Expose your people to the target you are trying to reach. Personal testimonies from those in your target group that focus on life transformation are a powerful reminder—and motivator—to us all. A few years ago at the Converge Great Lakes Annual Gathering in Milwaukee, a dear woman stood up and gave her testimony of how God used a new Converge Great Lakes church plant to reach her at her lowest point of despair and to deliver her out of years of abuse and other horrors. Many others spoke, and her talk only lasted ten minutes, but she received the only standing ovation, and I'm sure that everyone there still remembers her story. Even though the Gathering was just getting started, I could have said the benediction, and we could have gone home right after her talk.

Principle #2: Keep the facts in front of your people. It's difficult to argue with the facts. Using assessment tools to identify where your ministry stands and what your current needs are will help you supplement the story you are telling with an objective sense of reality. Several good tools are available. In the last chapter I mentioned the Percept Group,[41] an organization that provides an online tool for measuring the demographics and psychographics of your target area.

Additionally, Natural Church Development (NCD)[42] provides an assessment tool that permits you to objectively measure the strengths and weaknesses of your church ministry. As people are clearly able to see the needs and the vision, there is an increased urgency to get back on mission.

---

41 .http://www.perceptgroup.com/ Accessed 14 March 2012
42 See http://www.ncd-international.org/public/essence. html (accessed 16 March 2012)

Principle #3: Don't be afraid to share with passion. Many of us who are in full-time vocational ministry are too careful to not offend. Why? Not only do we want to avoid offending, but we know that dollars flow in or flow out based on how people feel about us. This sometimes causes us to hold back and not share the truth with passion. But, in my opinion, a lack of transparency squelches the work of the Holy Spirit.

Principle #4: Give your people firsthand experience. Give them a touch of the target community, or connect them with the persons you are trying to reach, especially when it allows those you lead to experience firsthand the need that you are seeking to keep before them. This is especially true for those who are 30 and under. They experience a global perspective of reaching their world for Christ not simply by giving money, as their grandparents did, nor by hearing stories, as their parents did, but by experience. This is why short-term experiences on the mission field, whether it be overseas or next door, are so very important for this generation. And they can be valuable for any generation. Prior to my 2008 trip to Ukraine, I had heard about the people of the Ukraine, and I was familiar with our ministries there. But not until I actually had boots on the ground, did my heart break for the needs of the people of Ukraine. This is what motivated me to act and create a strategic partnership between my district and the Sumy District of Ukraine.

Principle #5: Take time to invest in people. Relational investment always creates a wider door to be heard and a greater readiness to receive what is being shared. Too many leaders operate, however, out of the direct / dictate motif instead of the model / mentor motif. In the past, I have made the critical mistake of trying to lead with vision, not taking the time to create a sense of urgency by investing in relationships. I know when I am doing this because I come across as trying to sell someone on a program instead of giving that person an opportunity to be, and go, where God is moving. In order to create a sense of urgency you, as a turnaround leader, must be willing to spend time with the people you are leading. Only by doing this will your people grasp your sense of urgency. Even though the model / mentor motif is more time and energy consuming, I am convinced that it is not only more effective, but also closer to the leadership paradigm exercised by Jesus Christ.

In the model / mentor motif, you demonstrate the principle before you teach it to those you lead. You then create situations that allow those you lead to experience the truth you are seeking to convey. Then you debrief your protege to determine what he or she has intuitively learned through the experience. Then you bring your perspective as a mentor into the conversation. How do you do this to create a sense of urgency? At times you may need to allow things to fall apart a little bit so that those who are under your care will have a greater readiness to hear your perspective on how the situation can be addressed. In addition, they experience the sense of urgency firsthand.

One last word of warning: Many younger leaders do not spend the time needed to create a sense of urgency. They move straight to diagnosis and implementation. The result? They find it hard to sustain the initial momentum since it is so leader-driven. The values and the urgency of the situation are not shared by others who could continue creating and implementing the vision and enlarge the human capacity to move forward with constructive change.

Take the time to prayerfully create a clear sense of urgency in your ministry. If you do, the people you lead will not only embrace your clarion call, but they will follow through with the staying power to turn your vision into reality.

Pause to Ponder

Why is it important for you, as a turnaround ministry leader, to create a sense of urgency?

What role should the use of real life story play in your creating a sense of urgency within your particular ministry?

What role should explaining the downside of a situation play in creating a sense of urgency? Is it ever appropriate to divulge confidential information about either people, or a situation, in order to communicate the need and create a greater sense of urgency?

Chapter Five

Identify the Bottom Line

Find your rally point

Once you, as a turnaround leader, have hit rock bottom,[43] assessed the situation, and created a sense of urgency, you must next figure out the bottom line missional component around which your ministry will rally. This rally point is critical. If you aim at the wrong bull's eye, you will go down the wrong path, regardless of everything else you might be doing right.

In leadership literature, authors use a variety of phrases to label this missional rally point. Jim Collins, in his book *Good to Great*[44], calls it the organization's *Hedgehog Principle*. Will Mancini, in his wonderful book, *Church Unique*,[45] calls it

---

43 Knowing beyond a shadow of a doubt that, "Unless the LORD builds the house, they labor in vain who build it " Psalm 127:1 NASB

44 Jim Collins, *Good to Great: Why Some Companies Make the Leap ... And Others Don't* (New York: HarperBusiness, 2001).

45 Will Mancini, *Church Unique: How Missional Leaders*

his *Kingdom Concept.* John Kotter, in the book, *Leading Change*[46] (previously quoted), describes this rally point as the organization's *Vision.*

Different words, but they all mean basically the same thing. God has called your ministry in this season to accomplish something—unique to your ministry—within God's grand and comprehensive plan to reach the world for Christ. What is that calling? What is that rally point?

Keep the main thing the main thing

You need to know your ministry's rally point because you need to keep the main thing the main thing. This is so important, particularly for younger leaders. You must not be driven by your life circumstances or by the circumstances of others. Instead, you must remain focused on your sense of mission and purpose.

Several years ago, I read a powerful book entitled the *On-Purpose Person.*[47] Allow me to quote from this little book:

Cast Vision, Capture Culture, and Create Movement (Hoboken: Jossey-Bass / Wiley, 2008).

46 John P. Kotter, *Leading Change* (Boston: Harvard Business Review Press, 1996).

47 Kevin W. McCarthy, *The On-Purpose Person: Making Your Life Make Sense* (Madison, TN: On-Purpose Publishing, 2008).

Once there was a successful person. In fact he was more than successful his life had meaning and purpose. He was investing his time on earth wisely and making a significant difference in other people's lives. He had come to terms with himself; he knew his strengths and managed around his weaknesses. Every day was a fresh opportunity to become a better person...But it hadn't always been this way. He carried memories of frustration when his life had no meaning or purpose. Then "living" was just going through the motions stretched out along a string of days reacting to circumstances and people. Flashes of clarity were too often blurred by urgencies. There was no true focus or knowing who he really was. He was not in control and his own person. That was many years ago. Things are different now. He had learned a great deal since then and had put it into practice. He had learned to be on-purpose.

The central thesis of this book is this: Unless I develop a clear sense of self-awareness and self-identity, I will not know who I am, nor will I be able to clearly fulfill the purposes God has put me on this earth to fulfill.[48] As a result, I will live my

---

48 Ephesians 2:10

life dabbling in many things, but not accomplishing the one or two great things God has called me to do.

Jesus, the Apostle Paul, and all great men and women of God live their lives with a clear sense of purpose and mission. Paul said it like this, "But whatever things were gain to me, those things I have counted as loss for the sake of Christ. More than that, I count all things to be loss in view of the surpassing value of knowing Christ Jesus my Lord, for whom I have suffered the loss of all things, and count them but rubbish so that I may gain Christ …"[49] Jesus said, "For I have come down from heaven, not to do My own will, but the will of Him who sent Me."[50]

How to identify your ministry's rally point

Clarifying vision or mission for an individual is one thing, but to do it for an entire church or ministry is quite different. Begin by asking these four essential questions:

1. What are we doing that others are not only doing, but are doing better than us? What should we eliminate?

---

49 Philippians 3:7-8 NASB
50 John 6:38 NASB

2. What specific niche has God called us to play in His grand plan of redemption? Where should we focus?

3. How do our surroundings and the needs that God puts in our path figure into our corporate mission? How does our ministry context help define our focus?

4. How has God worked in our ministry in the past, and how does that give definition to our future? How does our historical context help define our focus?

Strategic vs. urgent Here we step away from the urgent and center on the strategic. This empowers you, as a turnaround leader, to lead from a proactive, future-oriented position. Turnaround leaders may need to put out fires. But if you are always putting out fires, you are leading from a reactionary position, and that is not a strong position to be in. Reactionary leadership will never take your ministry forward.

Narrow your focus Ministry leaders often fail to lead strategically because they try to do, and be, too much. This is particularly true of pastors. We forget to apply good New Testament biblical theology; namely, God never intended for your local church (or ministry) to be His whole body, but only an eye, or an ear, or a hand. Your ministry cannot be all things to all people. Church leaders were derailed back in the 1950s and 1960s when a consumer-oriented mentality sprang up. Local churches began seeking to provide the best programs, so each could attract more members. We fell into the trap of competing with one another, instead of helping each other build the Kingdom. Not only is this model not sustainable, but it also fails to take into account that people are no longer looking primarily for activities to do at church; rather, they are looking for relationships to build.

Steps to identifying your ministry's rally point

A process of discernment must take place before a clear missional vision emerges. This process should include the following:

1. Create a task force that not only guides this process but makes the recommendations to the leadership team first, and then helps the leader to communicate to the congregation and/or ministry constituents.

2. Look at what God has done in your ministry. Using primary sources such as

personal testimonial and face to face interviews, and secondary sources such as what others have written and said about your ministry, track where and how God has used your ministry to attract people to Christ, nurture them in their faith, and transform whole communities.

3. Hone in clearly on the specific needs in the community. Again, use both primary and secondary sources.

4. Get input from a broad of range of sources. This should be done through both written assessments, such as the NCD and Percept, and oral assessments such as interviews and focus groups.

5. Use empirical data (such as demographics and psychographics) to get an objective look at needs and strengths.

6. Set up times of prayer and fasting in order for these leaders to assess what God is up to in our midst.

7. Talk to other ministry leaders. Find out what they have done and/or are doing.

8. Immerse the entire process in prayer by rising up a prayer advancement team whose only responsibility is to pray for the

vision discernment process.

Do you have the will to follow through?

Once you have clarified the vision for your ministry, then comes the critical test: Are you willing to say no? Will you step away from things you have done, and done well, in the past in order to say yes to what God is calling you to do in the future? This is where the enemy will attack you most fiercely. Are you really willing to let your rally point influence every decision you make as a leader? Will you stay on track? Do you have the will to change? This is why creating urgency cannot be an afterthought but must be central to your task of organizational renewal. Creating urgency is critical because people are creatures of habit. They will not change, or even pay attention, unless someone communicates urgency.

Clarity of vision

Clarity of vision is critical to organizational renewal. If you don't know what you are shooting for, then it doesn't matter how fast—or how strong—you send out arrows. Every one will be a shot in the dark. Find your rally point, determine your vision, and live with the assurance that your ministry is advancing God's Kingdom purposes.

Pause to Ponder

Why is it so important to identify your ministry's rally point?

What are some of the hindrances to identifying your church's, or organization's, rally point?

How do you create broad ownership for the development of your ministry's particular rally point?

Chapter Six

Develop Your Core Strategies

Once your rally point is clearly defined, the next key activity for you, as a turnaround ministry leader, is to address and answer the how question. How will you accomplish your mission? What strategies will you employ? Strategy is another way of saying pathway or process by which you will achieve your desired outcome.

Four critical characteristics of effective strategies

Your strategy must be consistent with:

1. The ethos or values of the organization.

2. The context your ministry finds itself in.

3. The resource base of people and finances that your organization currently has available.

4. Clear and measurable outcomes.

The ethos principle

Your ministry's strategy must be consistent with the *ethos,* or values, of your organization. Your ministry's ethos is what gives it a particular "feel."

We see this in our individual lives, as well. Whether we realize it or not, all of us interpret life through a grid of mental images, emotions and interpretations. The writer of Proverbs put it this way, "Here's what matters most: Attend to what's inside your heart because the content of your heart will shape the direction of your life."[51]

Likewise, organizations develop a set of values. Your ministry's values are more than your theological beliefs, though values are indeed rooted in how you view God, His Word, and His plan of salvation. Values are the foundational building blocks upon which the organization builds its interactions with others.

For example, here are the core values of Converge Great Lakes:

We desire as a movement of churches to be:

- *Spiritually Dynamic*—We want our churches to be bibliocentric in their focus and God-

---

51 Proverbs 4:23 *The Easy Bible*® Used by permission.

focused in their sense of becoming communities of faith where the authority and
sufficiency of the Bible is paramount.

- *Relationally Devoted*—We want our churches to demonstrate the love of Christ to one
another, and not only to one another, but
also to a lost and dying world that
desperately needs Jesus.

- *Misionally Driven*—We want our churches
to not simply be a social club or a place
where friends congregate but a missional
community that wants to use all of its
people and financial resources to see men
and women, boys, and girls come to Christ
as Savior and Lord

- *Culturally Diverse*—We want our churches
to reflect the vast diversity of people
represented in the geographical boundaries
of Wisconsin and the UP of Michigan

- Generously Desirable—We want our
churches to be generous to those who are
part of their fellowship, as well as to those
who are not.

These five values drive everything we do as an
organization. They govern how we carry out our
clearly-defined mission: *"Converge Great Lakes*

exists to glorify God by strengthening churches so that they may reach those who do not know Jesus Christ locally, nearby, and around the world." Our ministry initiatives (our strategies), our resources, and our staffing all revolve around our values.

As a turnaround ministry leader, you will spend time on the front end, creating what I call a values-based culture and not a product-based culture. In other words, you never want to stoop to situational ethics. The ends do not justify the means.

How do you develop a values-based culture, as opposed to a products-based culture? A whole book could be written on that, but here are some insights that should be helpful.

Value insight #1: Do not reward behavior or attitudes that are not consistent with your values. Even leaders of Christian organizations can fall into what I call the "success syndrome." Sometimes we become so taken by a person's "success" that we overlook, or excuse, a lack of congruency in values. Why do we do this? Perhaps we are wowed by numbers and titles. Or perhaps we fail to understand the role of righteous indignation in the Christian life. When we fail to confront when confrontation is needed, we take a passive-aggressive stance in which we remain silent when we should speak up, all the while seething with anger on the inside.

I have a good friend who struggles with this type of confrontational style. Whenever a conflict comes up, instead of meeting the issue head on, he tends to bury it until he no longer can bury it. Then he explodes. The passive-aggressive person will subtly undercut what you might be doing by not sharing his or her views openly and honestly. Instead, this person will resist your leadership every step of the way through lack of follow-through, side comments or spreading disapproval behind your back, instead of confronting you head-on (The passive-evasive person, on the other hand, not only buries it, but never seeks to address the issue).

Value insight #2: Reward behavior and attitudes that are consistent with the values of the organization. As my wife would say, "Duh! Of course!" But even though rewarding behavior makes sense, many of us tend to overlook persons who are representing Christ and doing their job well because we are a crisis-orientated people. If it isn't broken, we do not tend to pay attention to it. But I have found that one way to substantially increase the performance of my staff is to pay attention to those whose behavior is consistent with the values of our organization by complimenting and rewarding that performance.

Value insight #3: Model what you want lived out. Jesus said, "A pupil is not above his teacher; but everyone, after he has been fully trained, will be like his teacher."[52] Paul puts it this way, "For you yourselves know how you ought to follow our example, because we did not act in an undisciplined manner among you, nor did we eat anyone's bread without paying for it, but with labor and hardship we kept working night and day so that we would not be a burden to any of you; not because we do not have the right to this, but in order to offer ourselves as a model for you, so that you would follow our example. "[53]

On February 3, 1994, Mother Teresa spoke at the National Prayer Breakfast with then President Bill Clinton, Vice President Al Gore, and their wives in attendance. During her address, she lambasted the evil of abortion and declared that it went against the heart of God. It was obvious to all that

---

52 Luke 6:40 NASB
53 2 Thessalonians 3:7-9 NASB

the President was uncomfortable. When questioned by the media afterward, President Clinton's only response was, "I cannot argue with a life so well-lived."

Value insight #4: Make ministry values a prayer priority. Once again I come back to the reality that the turnaround ministry leader must be so broken before God that prayer saturates everything. Identifying and adhering to your ministry's values becomes a prayer priority. We must understand, as church and ministry leaders, that we do not wrestle with flesh and blood but against spiritual forces of darkness[54] who want to keep our churches and mission agencies so derailed and self-absorbed that the Great Commission—the task God has called us to accomplish—falls by the way side. But the Apostle John assures us, "This is the confidence which we have before Him, that, if we ask anything according to His will, He hears us. And if we know that He hears us in whatever we ask, we know that we have the requests which we have asked from Him."[55]

---

54 Ephesians 6:12
55 1 John 5:14-15 NASB

The context principle

Strategies not only must be consistent with the ethos or values of the organization, they must also be consistent with the context in which the ministry functions.

Cross-cultural missionaries call this *contextualization.* Contextualization means translating the gospel in both word and deed into a language and a lifestyle consistent with the people we are trying to reach. We understand the importance of this in an overseas missionary context. But sometimes we completely miss the importance of this here in the United States. Rather than figure out how to "do church" in a way that reaches the target group we have been sent to reach—our mission field—we sometimes fight with each other over our insistence on doing church the way we are most comfortable doing it. It doesn't do any good to satisfy the saints if we don't connect with those around us that we are trying to reach for Christ. We need to remember that we are on a mission field, and we have an enemy who rejoices when we fight against each other instead of focusing on reaching people for Christ.

When our strategies thus are not consistent with the people we are trying to reach, we will not be effective, no matter how hard we work, pray or fast. Again and again I have seen this reality played out. Early in my ministry, I unknowingly violated the context principle. We began a church in Chicago and saw rapid growth for the first two years. Then we reached a crossroads. We outgrew the building we were leasing. Through a number of circumstances, we decided to purchase a large, but old, church building in the heart of one of the worst project developments in the city. Now, please hear this next statement clearly: The projects need ministry just like the more affluent part of the city and the suburbs need ministry. They just did not need ministry from us. We were, at our core, a group of upwardly-mobile, middle-class African Americans whose experience was totally different from the people we were trying to reach. Our growth not only stopped once we moved into this new facility, it actually declined because our strategies, and who we were culturally, were not a fit for this context. The story had a happy ending, however. This church eventually merged with another church, moved into a middle-class, working-class area on the southside of Chicago, and is thriving today.

Strategies thus must be consistent with the context that the ministry finds it in.

The resources principle

In addition to following the ethos and context principles, our strategies must be reflective of, and consistent with, the resources that God has provided. By resources, I mean both people and material / financial resources. In other words, we must live within our means. At the same time, we exercise a holy faith that God will supply what our ministry needs if we are accomplishing what He has called us to accomplish.

In my view, too many ministries make the grave mistake—in the name of faith—of spending more money than they have, or could ever hope to have, and they turn their ministry into nothing more than a conduit to take in more money in order to keep the machine going, regardless of the results. But God cannot bless a ministry with provision if we are not being faithful to wisely steward the resources He has already entrusted to our care. Too many churches are operating in the "what if" syndrome—what if we had more of this or more of that? But living within our means is a test to see how effectively we can manage what God has already entrusted to us.

Our strategies must be developed with resourcing in mind. Resources should not hinder the outworking of our ministry, but they can be used by God to show us where: (1) we are not trusting him enough; or (2) we are mismanaging what He has already entrusted to us. God will not multiply what we have until we learn how to steward properly what we have been given.

The outcomes principle.

Finally, strategies must be harnessed to clear and measurable outcomes. While your rally point answers the question, "Where are we going?," your strategies answer the question, "How are we going to get there?" Obviously, you have no way of knowing whether your strategies are any good if you cannot measure the progress they empower. Someone put it like this, "If you cannot measure it, it must not be worth much."[56]

Am I saying that we should put God in a box or operate a ministry just like a business? No. God is free to be God … always. But God is also a God of process, of order, of evaluation. Remember, all the way back to the first chapter of Genesis, we find God using evaluative criteria to describe His creation.

What are the mile markers on the path to your destination? How will you know if you're moving

---

56 Source unknown.

forward? These questions need to be answered.

Developing clear and measurable objectives by which you gauge your ministry's effectiveness does three things for you as a turnaround ministry leader:

1. It gives you hope. It helps you and your team to rejoice when you see clear and measurable progress.

2. It gives you wisdom. Because you are going through a process to make your decisions, instead of just making decisions on a whim, you can be wise and prayerful about how you use God's resources. This gives God more room to work.

3. It empowers you to recruit "on purpose" leaders who not only want to know where your ministry is going, but also how it intends to get there.

Turnaround ministry leaders connect their rally point with clearly definable strategies that can be measured.

Pause to Ponder

What was your reaction to the "ethos principle"? What role do you feel organizational values should play in the outworking of a church's or organization's rally point?

Discuss, with a close colleague in your organization, value insight number one in terms of not rewarding behavior that does not conform to the values of an organization. What hinders us from not speaking the truth in love to those around us whose behavior does not reflect the values of our organizations?

How important is it for church or ministry leaders to take into account the context from which their core strategies must be implemented?

Chapter Seven

Get the Wrong People off the Bus, and Get the Right People on the Bus

According to world-renowned leadership expert Jim Collins, even if you are clear on where you want to go, and understand how you intend to get there, you still will not turn your ministry around until you get the right people on the bus and the wrong people off the bus. In his book, *Good to Great*, he writes:

> When we began the research project, we expected to find that the new first step in taking a company from good to great would be to set a new direction, a new vision and strategy for the company, and then get people committed and aligned behind that new direction. We found something quite the opposite. The executives who ignited the transformation from good to great did not first figure out where to drive the bus and then get people to take it there. No, they first got the right people on the bus (and the wrong people off the bus) and then

figured out where to drive it. They said, in essence, "Look, I don't really know where we should take this bus. But I know this much: If we get the right people on the bus, the right people in the right seats, and the wrong people off the bus, then we'll figure out how to take it someplace great."[57]

After almost four decades of ministry experience, I say, "Amen!" I have seen churches and ministries flourish when it seemed like they did not have the slickest strategic plan and others that were right out of Madison Avenue who were going nowhere because of the people they had on the bus.

How to identify if someone is on the right bus

What do we mean when we say the wrong people versus the right people? In most cases, we're not talking about character deficiencies. However, sometimes character issues are a problem. Sometimes, as Christ followers, we try to do everything possible to avoid dealing with the issues that need to be confronted. But we need to remember that sometimes the greatest way to love someone is to gently restore that person.[58]

---

57 Jim Collins, *Good to Great: Why Some Companies Make the Leap … And Others Don't* (New York: HarperBusiness, 2001).

58 Galatians 6:1

Remember that Jesus was not only full of grace, but also truth.[59] Likewise, we need to "speak the truth in love."[60] If there is a sin problem or character weakness, that needs to be addressed.

However, in most cases, I'm talking about the person whose gifting, passion, experience and training are not a right fit for the role they have been assigned in your ministry. Or, in some cases, the person has been called to help another bus move in a God-given direction. As a result, that person should not be occupying space and time on your bus using his or her relational or positional influence to pull your ministry off into a different direction that God had not intended.

Here are some questions that I now ask as I converse with people—especially when I am considering them for leadership. I wish I would have had these talks thirty-five years ago. They would have saved a lot of crashes.

1. Do the people on my bus buy into the vision?

2. Do the people on my bus characterize and live out, with passion, the values of the organization?

---

59 John 1:14
60 Ephesians 4:15

3. Do the people on the bus have the necessary gifting, training and experience to perform their role in a superior manner?

4. Do the people on my bus have the spiritual maturity and character to respond biblically when things do fall apart?

Why don't people perform up to their potential? This is a question I have pondered deeply over the last 36 years. Here are the four biggest reasons I have identified. People do not perform up to their capabilities because the job they have been called to do:

1. Does not match their capabilities and gifting.

2. Involves people with whom they are not in sync.

3. Does not resource them well enough to allow them to accomplish all they have been asked to do.

4. Has not been carefully designed so that clear and measurable outcomes are up front clearly seen and agreed upon by all parties.

In his book, *The Making of a Leader,*[61] Dr. Robert Clinton describes the time in a leader's life when he/she reaches what Dr. Clinton calls *congruence.* Congruence happens when all of our experiences, all our gifting, and all of our training come together in our vocational calling so that there is a ministry match. All of us have a longing for significance. All of us have a longing to make an eternal difference. All of us want to know that this existence here on this earth is more than just us taking up space and passing time. Unfortunately, many never experience congruence.

Congruence is not just key for the individual. It's key for your ministry. The more you can plug people into their place of congruence, the faster your ministry will move toward your vision— assuming you have the right people on your bus. But, if the wrong people are on your bus, no amount of congruence will help because they are moving in a different direction.

How do you find the right people?

Finding the right people is critical to the turnaround process. As a senior leader, here's

---

61 Robert Clinton, *The Making of a Leader: Recognizing the Lessons and Stages of Leadership Development,* Colorado Springs: NavPress, 1988).

what you need to keep in focus when recruiting and hiring:

1. Find people who love the vision and mission of your ministry. Find a candidate who is willing to invest time, gifts, talents and treasures to help you take your ministry to its desired outcome.

2. Hire competence, specifically the competence needed to empower you to accomplish your mission. Your new team member needs to possess the skills that you need to lead the ministry in the correct direction. Remember that track record trumps formal credentials. The right education is great, and usually necessary, but review what the person has actually done.

3. Character is critical. Do an in-depth reference check (Contact me for more information on how to carry out the reference check process). Your new team member needs to possess the character necessary to endure hardship as your ministry moves in the direction it needs to move. Do not sacrifice character for the sake of expediency. Do not mistake personality for character, or gifting for

character. Do not sacrifice character simply because you like the candidate. Remember, character is who we are when no one is looking.

4. Hire teachability. Find people who make themselves available to be led. Teachability is critical for a leadership team to thrive and function well with one another. The Apostle Paul said, "be subject to one another in the fear of Christ."[62] Mutual submission is a hallmark characteristic of leaders who can be used to turn around churches and ministry organizations.

5. Find people that fit who you are as a leader, especially if they are going to be in key ministry roles. Some people call this chemistry. I like to call this ministry match. They need to be compatible with your personality. Do not underestimate the importance of this. Many wonderful partnerships begin in a blaze of glory but end in conflict because this area is not considered. How do you evaluate ministry match? Use personality tests such as

---

62 Ephesians 5:21 NASB

Strengths Finders[63], Myers Briggs[64], or Conflict Style Assessment.[65]

Helping people off the bus

Not only do you need to get the right people on the bus, but you need to get the wrong people off the bus. Many people labor under the assumption that Christian-based organizations must put up with people who are not the right fit. This is a fallacy. You do not. If someone is mismatched to their role or not a good fit for your ministry, or if there are character or attitudinal issues that cannot be resolved, that person needs to find a new opportunity elsewhere. Even though it seems painful—and at times it is painful, out counseling someone who is not the right fit is the most loving thing you can do for that person and for your organization.

---

63 Tom Rath, *StrengthsFinder 2.0* (New York: Gallup Press, 2007).
64 http://www.myersbriggs.org/ (accessed 7 April 2012)
65 See http://www.churchsmart.com/SearchResults.asp?Search=conflict+style+assessment (accessed 9 April 2012). See also Jim Van Yperen, *Making Peace: A Guide to Overcoming Church Conflict* (Chicago: Moody Publishers, 2002).

Evaluation

Many people resist the idea of bringing evaluation into a church or ministry, particularly the evaluation of volunteers. But there is no reason that employees and volunteers who are doing Kingdom work should be held to a lower standard of accountability than those who are in the secular workplace.

Developing a system for your ministry

How do you develop a system that: (1) honors God; (2) affirms the dignity of those you lead; (3) helps you identify who is, and who is not, a good fit; and (4) helps you transition those who are on the wrong bus and need to move on?

Here are a few suggestions:

#1: Application / References Bring people (including volunteers) into your ministry with care. Do that job right. At minimum, insist on an application process, and make sure you check references. At higher levels of responsibility, consider including testing to see, in detail, the gifting and personality of the person being brought into your organization.

#2: Orientation Make sure you do some type of orientation that clearly outlines not only what the job is, but also when and how the employee or volunteer (yes, even volunteers) will be evaluated. The broader the scope of responsibility, the more in-depth the orientation.

#3: Job Description Make sure all paid and non-paid staff[66] have clear job descriptions and that those expectations are consistently followed.

#4: Evaluation Develop an evaluation system. It should: (1) be rooted in the job description; (2) be designed around clear and measurable job outcomes; and (3) allow the employee or volunteer to provide a self-evaluation, in addition to an evaluation by a supervisor.

#5: Communication Address both performance and attitudinal deficiencies as soon as they become evident. Keeping short accounts with those we serve will usually short circuit major conflict.

---

66 I consider all people staff who serve the church or ministry because they represent God and the church to others.

#6: Confrontation If a team member's behavior warrants loving, but firm, confrontation, don't shy away. When you do confront, be clear about what observable behavior you are confronting. Give examples, and explain why this behavior does not represent the values of your organization and / or how it hinders the mission of your ministry.

#7: Review Use the annual review[67] as a means to document progress—behavior that reflects the value and furthers the vision of your ministry. But also, if warranted, document personal or professional behavior that needs to be changed because it does not reflect the values or further the mission of your organization.

#8: Release If repeated and documented behaviors do not reflect the values of your ministry and / or are not helping to move your ministry toward its vision, or if the person is no longer a good fit for the position,[68] then release may be necessary. Start by getting counsel—

---

67 In some cases, depending on the role, you will have a semiannual checkup along with the official annual review.

68 Sometimes the person outgrows the job; sometimes the job outgrows the person in it.

including, if appropriate, legal advice. If everything points toward ending this person's role in your organization, then follow a clearly established protocol to out counsel this person. Follow the same protocol if you release a volunteer. Understand that, in some cases, you may need to terminate a program, and that may be a necessary price for making sure you have the right people on the bus. If the process is done correctly, your decision should not come as a surprise to the person being released, except in those cases where a financial downturn requires a trimming of staff. A predetermined process needs to be in place for these situations. If a separation becomes necessary, this process should be followed. Make sure that checkpoints have been adhered to and proper documentation has been collected along the way. Make sure that the process clearly outlines why separation is necessary.

Concern about how others will view the separation is important. However, this concern should never paralyze a leader if separation is best for the organization. But be sure to follow a well-defined protocol, and keep proper documentation in case legal challenges come about as a result of the separation.

Pause to Ponder

Ask yourself the question: Who are the right persons for the particular ministry bus you are currently on? What was the result of your reflection on this question?

Do you agree that leaders need to find others who are not only competent but also are a "fit"? What is your response to the concept of "fit"?

Have you ever had to transition someone out of a position, whether in the church or in business? How did this make you feel? Do you feel it is right for church and ministry leaders to come to a place where they should intentionally "get people off the bus"?

Chapter Eight

Principle-Centered Leadership vs. Perception-Centered Leadership

Being broken before God, finding your ministry's rally point, creating a values-based culture, and getting the right people on the bus are all critical to turnaround ministry leadership. But, without principle-centered leadership, any progress you make will soon be lost.

What is principle-centered leadership? Stephen Covey introduced this concept to me in his book, *Principle-Centered Leadership.*[69] Though published in 1992, it is just as relevant today as it was the day it first came out. "Principle-centered power is created when the values of the follower and leader overlap. Control is apparent, but it is not external; it is self-control. It elicits a willingness to risk doing the right things because they are valued and modeled by the leader. People follow the leader because of who he or she is."

---

69 Stephen R. Covey, *Principle-Centered Leadership* (Los Angeles: Fireside Press, 1992).

In thinking about the above definition, four clear contrasts come to my mind:

- *Principled-centered leaders* lead from core convictions.

- *Perception-centered leaders* lead from public opinion polls.

- *Principled-centered leaders* lead from their deep passion for the mission.

- *Perception-centered leaders* lead from a deep passion to please others.

- *Principled-centered leaders* lead form a deep commitment to do whatever is necessary for the betterment of the organization.

- *Perception-centered leaders* lead from a deep commitment to do whatever is best for them.

- *Principled-centered leaders* model what they preach more than they preach it.

- *Perception-centered leaders* are more

concerned with how something looks than how it is.

These four contrasts boil down the differences between a principle-centered leader and a perception-centered leader. Allow me to elaborate on each of them.

Contrast #1: Leading from core convictions instead of public opinion polls

Core convictions are deep inner values that drive a person. They make you who you are. Who you are is not what everyone sees, but what God sees when no one else is around. These convictions are non-negotiable perspectives that give you a sense of self and define who you really are. "For as he thinketh in his heart, so is he ..."[70] These values are generally built into the fabric of a person's character by age six or seven. They influence your world view, including how you view yourself. These foundational values can be shaken through a traumatic event or through conversion and genuine repentance. Making Christ the Lord of your life creates a change of mind (repentance) that sends you in a different direction.

---

70 Proverbs 23:7a KJV

Here God's word plays a foundational role in the life of the believer. A person may trust Christ as Savior, yet live out his or her former manner of life, unless the values and convictions of scripture are allowed to reshape the mind and heart. Paul admonished his son in the faith, Timothy, with these words, "You, however, continue in the things you have learned and become convinced of, knowing from whom you have learned them, and that from childhood you have known the sacred writings which are able to give you the wisdom that leads to salvation through faith which is in Christ Jesus. All Scripture is inspired by God and profitable for teaching, for reproof, for correction, for training in righteousness; so that the man of God may be adequate, equipped for every good work."[71] Note the words "convinced of." These core values govern how you perceive yourself and how you act when challenges and trials come into your life. When we get "bumped" by life, what's inside comes out. As Jesus said, "It is not what enters into the mouth that defiles the man, but what proceeds out of the mouth, this defiles the man."[72] Core convictions control our responses in life. They need to be based on unchangeable truths.

---

71 2 Timothy 3:14-17 NASB
72 Matthew 15:11 NASB

Principle-centered leaders are individuals who would rather lose their following than lose themselves. Principle-centered leaders ask the question, "Is this right?," rather than asking, "What will people think if I do this?" Principle-centered leaders would rather lose an election than compromise their character.

In my opinion, it is impossible for any organization to truly turn around without principle-centered leaders sprinkled throughout the organization who walk in their core convictions, rather than chase public opinion polls.

I am not saying what others think is not important. Any good leader is always aware of what the people she is leading think and feel about a particular direction. However, at the end of the day, the "what is right?" question trumps all other considerations.

Contrast #2: Accomplishing the mission instead of merely pleasing people

Their mission, not themselves, not their own personal agenda, not the agenda of a few friends or colleagues, is paramount in the minds and hearts of all principle-centered leaders.

Vince Lombardi, the Super Bowl-winning coach of the Green Bay Packers, was a man who lived his life with his goal, or his sense of mission, as the overriding factor in his life. He said it this way, "Winning isn't everything. The will to win is the only thing."[73]

Because ministry is a people-helping and people-centered profession, it is tempting for ministry leaders to put pleasing people ahead of pleasing God. Yes, we care about people. But how people feel about us is not the bottom line. Ultimately, our standards are the Great Commandment[74] and the Great Commission.[75]

The story of Pontius Pilate is one of the most unfortunate examples of a perception-centered

73 See http://en.wikipedia.org/wiki/Winning_isn%27t_everything;_it%27s_the_only_thing (accessed 11 April 2012) quoting James A. Michener, Sports in America (New York: Fawcett/Random House, 1987).
74 And He said to him, "'YOU SHALL LOVE THE LORD YOUR GOD WITH ALL YOUR HEART, AND WITH ALL YOUR SOUL, AND WITH ALL YOUR MIND.' This is the great and foremost commandment. The second is like it, 'YOU SHALL LOVE YOUR NEIGHBOR AS YOURSELF.'" Matthew 22:37-39 NASB
75 And Jesus came up and spoke to them, saying, "All authority has been given to Me in heaven and on earth. Go therefore and make disciples of all the nations, baptizing them in the name of the Father and the Son and the Holy Spirit, teaching them to observe all that I commanded you; and lo, I am with you always, even to the end of the age." Matthew 28:18-20 NASB

leader who bowed to the wishes and whims of the people instead of doing what he knew was right. As a result, he will go down in history as the man who crucified Jesus.

Consider this instructive passage from the Gospel of Matthew:

> Now Jesus stood before the governor, and the governor questioned Him, saying, "Are You the King of the Jews?" And Jesus said to him, "It is as you say." And while He was being accused by the chief priests and elders, He did not answer. Then Pilate said to Him, "Do You not hear how many things they testify against You?" And He did not answer him with regard to even a single charge, so the governor was quite amazed. Now at the feast the governor was accustomed to release for the people any one prisoner whom they wanted. At that time they were holding a notorious prisoner, called Barabbas. So when the people gathered together, Pilate said to them, "Whom do you want me to release for you? Barabbas, or Jesus who is called Christ?" For he knew that because of envy they had handed Him over. While he was sitting on the judgment seat, his wife sent him a message, saying, "Have nothing to do with that righteous Man; for last night I suffered greatly in a dream because of Him." But the chief priests and the elders

persuaded the crowds to ask for Barabbas and to put Jesus to death. But the governor said to them, "Which of the two do you want me to release for you?" And they said, "Barabbas." Pilate said to them, "Then what shall I do with Jesus who is called Christ?" They all said, "Crucify Him!" And he said, "Why, what evil has He done?" But they kept shouting all the more, saying, "Crucify Him!" When Pilate saw that he was accomplishing nothing, but rather that a riot was starting, he took water and washed his hands in front of the crowd, saying, "I am innocent of this Man's blood; see to that yourselves." And all the people said, "His blood shall be on us and on our children!" Then he released Barabbas for them; but after having Jesus scourged, he handed Him over to be crucified.[76]

I gather three lessons from this little narrative:

Lesson #1: Even though Pilate knew that there was nothing legitimate against Jesus, he still persisted in crucifying him because the cries of the crowd were more influential than the cries of his conscience.

Lesson #2: Even when God tried to speak to him directly and through others (his wife), he still

---

76 Matthew 27:11-26 NASB

refused to hear the voice of God because the voice of the people had drowned out God's voice.

Lesson #3: Even though he knew Jesus was innocent, he failed to take a principled stand because he feared disappointing an influential part of his constituency. Instead, he chose to travel the path of least resistance. He made a decision that had nothing to do with the question of what is right but only what concerned what was expedient for him.

Principle-centered leaders lead from a deep commitment to the mission instead of a frantic desire to please others.

Contrast #3: Doing what's best for the organization, not what's best for themselves

Principle-centered leaders are motivated to do whatever it takes (within legal and ethical boundaries) for the betterment of the organization while perception-centered leaders, at the end of the day, are committed to do whatever is best for themselves. Principle-centered leaders take this high road because they hold the core belief that what they are doing is right and that the mission that they are seeking to accomplish is worthy of their sacrifice.

Several years ago, we saw this attitude play out before us in the rescuing of Marine Jessica Lynch. Jessica, who had fought bravely for this country, had been captured by the Iraq military. A few days later, our special forces conducted a daring and successful rescue operation. This operation was later turned into a made-for-TV movie. During the movie, one of our Marines answered the question, "Why did you undertake such a dangerous mission?" His answer was simple, "We will never leave a fallen comrade."[77]

This core belief of doing whatever it takes to see the organization succeed is not just necessary in the military. It is necessary in all phases of life, and especially in the greatest mission of all time— that of seeing men and women, boys and girls, come to know Christ as Savior and Lord. Given the eternal impact of what we do in ministry, all other undertakings pale in comparison.

This core belief has eroded, however, especially in the last fifty years. This is, in part, due to our response to the prosperity we have had the privilege of enjoying. In some ways, we have become like the church of Laodicea[78] who, in their wealth, became lukewarm in their faith. Here in

---

77 http://articles.latimes.com/2003/apr/04/news/war-
    lynch4 Accessed 24 May 2012.
78 See Revelation 3:14-22.

America, we have the biggest church buildings and the most money, yet we are often stagnant in pursuing the Great Commission and in our willingness to do whatever it takes to see this mission accomplished. By contrast, in large portions of the world, the church flourishes despite persecution and poverty. Why? Leaders care more about the mission than they do about their very lives.

Contrast #4: Modeling what you preach instead of keeping up appearances

Principle-centered leaders model what they preach instead of focusing on how something is going to come across. Jesus instructed His followers, "Let your light shine before men in such a way that they may see your good works, and glorify your Father who is in heaven."[79] But to those who were just trying to put on a show, He said, "Woe to you, scribes and Pharisees, hypocrites! For you are like whitewashed tombs which on the outside appear beautiful, but inside they are full of dead men's bones and all uncleanness."[80]

Our ability to lead is not dependent on what we

79 Matthew 5:16 NASB
80 Matthew 23:27 NASB

say but on what people see. When they see an authentic, broken Christ follower who exudes the life of Jesus, this motivates them to follow that leader—not because of who he is but because of the Christ they see in him. Paul said, "Be imitators of me, just as I also am of Christ. "[81] Peter put it this way, "shepherd the flock of God among you, exercising oversight not under compulsion, but voluntarily, according to the will of God; and not for sordid gain, but with eagerness; nor yet as lording it over those allotted to your charge, but proving to be examples to the flock. "[82]

In contrast, perception-centered leaders are more concerned with how something is going to come across—not whether what people see is truly genuine. They only care about impression, not substance. The principle-centered leader lives out, and models, his or her core convictions in a way that is transparent and authentic. Perception-based leaders impress people for a while, but eventually what is buried inside does come out.

Turnaround ministry leaders who are being used

---

81 1 Corinthians 11:1 NASB
82 1 Peter 5:2-3 NASB

to transform ministries exhibit a principle-centered life. They care about living out their core convictions, instead of focusing on winning popularity contests. They are more concerned about the mission than they are about pleasing people. They value their people above themselves, and they model authentic godliness, rather than going around trying to make a good impression. Principle-centered leaders, like Jesus, have always been—and will always be—the type of leaders that God's Spirit can move upon, and through, to accomplish His purposes on this earth.

Pause to Ponder

Describe, in your own words, what it means to lead from "core convictions." What is the personal risk to a leader who operates out of principle instead of convenience?

As you look at your own life, what have been some of the underlying reasons you have, at times, operated out of a mentality to "please people," even when you knew what was the principled, or right, thing to do?

React to the statement, "In contrast, perception-centered leaders are more concerned with how something is going to come across—not whether what people see is truly genuine."

Chapter Nine

Embrace Conflict

Conflict is the natural outcome of change

You are a turnaround ministry leader. That means you will be used by God to turn your ministry around. That can't be done without change. Where there is no change, there will be no conflict. However, where there is change, conflict is inevitable.

When two objects meet at the same place, one of them is going to have to move. Likewise, whenever change—large or small—is interjected into a situation, there will always be some kind of reaction. Change, and its pursuant and inevitable conflict, is a given. What is not a given is how well the change process will be managed. How well this process is managed will determine whether or not the conflict that ensues moves the organization forward or stymies its growth toward the accomplishment of its mission.

For most of us—there are exceptions—conflict is

not something we look forward to. How we experience conflict is greatly shaped by how conflict was handled in our family of origin and our own personal history with conflict. But Christ came to redeem this part of our lives, and we can learn strategies to manage conflict constructively and use it to spur the organization forward.

My own experience

Even though I have been in Christian ministry for nearly four decades, and even though I have held some major leadership roles, I, like most people, do not like conflict. Why is that? I think much of it has to do with my family of origin. My father was a violent and physically abusive man who mistreated my mother. Up until the day they separated (I was six or seven), I was exposed to all types of arguing and abusive behavior. To this day, I cringe when I think about it. This created in me a deep desire to have the approval and acceptance of my father. That transferred over to pleasing people and trying to settle arguments before they began by giving in and going along with whoever seemed to be the more dominant in the relationship. This tendency to appease is still with me today. It has hindered me greatly in dealing with people who need to be confronted. At times, I confess, I have internalized and tried to work around a situation instead of immediately dealing with it head-on. Understand that there is wisdom in being quick to listen, slow to speak, and slow to become angry.[83] God does want us to wait in order to get His perspective on the situation. However, sometimes my waiting would extend beyond the point of prudence, and the situation was not resolved in a timely manner. When that happens, things build up and sometimes blow up, creating more hurt, rather than less.

I share my personal journey with you in this area so that you will understand that all of us are in process. Being an effective turnaround leader doesn't require perfection, but it does require the courage to look honestly at ourselves, see our weaknesses, and turn to God for strength.

Out of this pain I have learned several key truths that have made this journey much better than it was twenty, ten, even five years ago.

Seven truths about conflict

Truth #1: Conflict in and of itself is not bad. Only when it is poorly managed can it become

---

83 James 1:19

destructive. That is why God's word is very clear. When there is a disagreement between two people, they should resolve it quickly and privately. If resolution doesn't quickly come about, there is a process of reconciliation.[84]

Truth #2: People resist change. Whenever change is introduced, there will be conflict. As people living in a fallen world, we are set in our ways more than we realize. Due to our sin nature, we like things to be done our way, regardless of whether our way is God's way or not. We need the power of God to intervene to produce a willingness to embrace change.

Truth #3: The real fight is with our spiritual enemy. Ultimately, our struggle is not against one another but against Satan and his desire to oppose God's agenda on this earth.[85]

Truth #4: Contain conflict. Meet directly with the person with whom you have the conflict. Don't involve others unless the two of you are unable to resolve this issue. Triangulation—involving others

---

84 See Matthew 5:23-26, 18:15-17
85 See Ephesians 6:12

who are not part of the problem nor part of the solution—escalates conflict and creates a much bigger mess to clean up. This is why Matthew 18:15-17 instructs us to start by going to the person in private.

Truth #5: Establish and follow protocols for conflict. Clear protocols need to be in place within a ministry context and followed so that conflict can be dealt with properly and to ensure that division does not spread. Within a church, for example, the protocols should address the following types of conflicts: member to member; member to pastor; pastor to other leader; pastor to other pastor; and non-believer outside of the congregation to a congregational member. The protocol should clearly spell out the goals of the conflict resolution process—what can and cannot be accomplished, the steps to be taken, how privacy and confidentiality should be handled, what is and is not admissable, the responsibilities of each party, the scriptural basis for your procedures, and the use of any assessment instruments. Contact me directly for more information.

Truth #6: Being in the right doesn't justify treating others poorly. We are commanded to speak the truth in love.[86] Yes, we should stand our ground in defense of the right principles. But there is a right way and a wrong way to do that. Keep this passage in mind: "But refuse foolish and ignorant speculations, knowing that they produce quarrels. The Lord's bond-servant must not be quarrelsome, but be kind to all, able to teach, patient when wronged, with gentleness correcting those who are in opposition, if perhaps God may grant them repentance leading to the knowledge of the truth, and they may come to their senses and escape from the snare of the devil, having been held captive by him to do his will."[87]

Truth #7: Prayer must be pervasive throughout the conflict. Only God can reveal truth, and only God can change hearts; therefore, we need to beseech the Lord of the Harvest to work on behalf of His glory and for His honor to bring about unity in the situation.[88]

Changing an organization that has plateaued, or

---

86 Ephesians 4:15
87 2 Timothy 2:23-26 NASB
88 See John 17:23

is experiencing decline, will bring about conflict. Conflict is inevitable. However, it does not need to be destructive if properly managed. My question to you is this: "Are you willing to personally pay the price of conflict for the sake of God's Kingdom?"

Pause to Ponder

React to the statement: "Conflict in and of itself is not bad." In what context is this statement true?

What is the relationship between conflict and our tendency to resist change?

Discuss Matthew 18:15-20 with a close friend. Do you see this being lived out within your local church / ministry community? If you do, why? If you do not, why not?

Chapter Ten

Now What?

No book, no matter what the size, can cover every possible scenario that you might face as a turnaround ministry leader. That's why I make myself available for personal and email consultation.

My services to you and your ministry may include, but are not limited to:

- conflict resolution

- assistance in developing your mission statement

- choosing appropriate assessment tools

- assisting with key staff selection

- assessment of your ministry's stage in the organizational life cycle

- providing tools and strategies for staff performance evaluation

- connecting, or renewing, your rally point with those you seek to serve.

Visit my website:

TurnaroundMinistryLeader.com

for more information. A list of further references and resources is also available at the website.

Feel free to email me at DwightPerry@msn.com. All email correspondence will be treated in confidence. Please allow seven days for response, as I will respond to each email personally.

May God bless you on your journey to becoming the turnaround ministry leader that God wants to use to accomplish His kingdom purposes for His glory!

Shalom!

Dr. Dwight Perry